Christian
Animism

Christian Animism

Shawn Sanford Beck

CHRISTIAN
ALTERNATIVE

Winchester, UK
Washington, USA

First published by Christian Alternative Books, 2015
Christian Alternative Books is an imprint of John Hunt Publishing Ltd.,
Laurel House, Station Approach,
Alresford, Hants, SO24 9JH, UK
office1@jhpbooks.net
www.johnhuntpublishing.com
www.christian-alternative.com

For distributor details and how to order please visit the 'Ordering' section on our website.

Text copyright: Shawn Sanford Beck 2014

ISBN: 978 1 78279 965 8
Library of Congress Control Number: 2014958362

A CIP catalogue record for this book is available from the British Library.

Design: Stuart Davies

Printed and bound by CPI Group (UK) Ltd, Croydon, CR0 4YY, UK

We operate a distinctive and ethical publishing philosophy in all areas of our business, from our global network of authors to production and worldwide distribution.

CONTENTS

Acknowledgements

To begin with, as in all things, glory must be given to the Triune One: Creator, Word, and Holy Sophia. A close second goes to my family, who put up with my eccentric ramblings on a regular basis. Thanks as well to Joel and Cheryl Mowchenko, and Derek Tannis, who offered hospitality of mind, body, and spirit for writing retreats. Much gratitude to Erika Faith, Michele Rowe, the St. Thomas Wesley reading group, the Sophian Grove of Rivendell, and my Sophian Druidry students for putting this material to the test of ongoing reflection and practice. And finally, to all the creatures of God's beloved web of creation: may She bless you and keep you, always.

Preface

They found that they were looking at a most extraordinary face. It belonged to a large Man-like, almost Troll-like, figure, at least fourteen foot high, very sturdy, with a tall head, and hardly any neck. Whether it was clad in stuff like green and grey bark, or whether that was its hide, was difficult to say. At any rate the arms, at a short distance from the trunk, were not wrinkled, but covered with a brown smooth skin. The large feet had seven toes each. The lower part of the long face was covered with a sweeping grey beard, bushy, almost twiggy at the roots, thin and mossy at the ends. But at the moment the hobbits noted little but the eyes. These deep eyes were now surveying them, slow and solemn, but very penetrating. They were brown, shot with a green light. Often afterwards Pippin tried to describe his first impression of them.

"One felt as if there was an enormous will behind them, filled up with the ages of memory and long, slow, steady thinking; but their surface was sparkling with the present; like sun shimmering on the outer leaves of a vast tree, or on the ripples of a very deep lake. I don't know, but it felt as if something that grew in the ground – asleep, you might say, or just feeling itself as something between root-tip and leaf-tip, between deep earth and sky had suddenly waked up, and was considering you with the same slow care that it had given to its own inside affairs for endless years." (The Two Towers, 452)

Unlike Pippin and Merry, two jolly young hobbits from Tolkien's Middle Earth, not many of us will be blessed in our lifetime with such a vivid and gripping encounter with an Ent, or "tree-shepherd". However, if we carefully search

1

out the recesses of memory, it is entirely possible that, at some point in our childhood, each of us was given a taste of the "aliveness", the sentience even, of the natural world around us. Perhaps it was a favourite tree in the backyard, or a special boulder in the field; maybe it was even a momentary glimpse of a faery, a water kelpie, or some other inhabitant of that mystic land just beneath the surface of things. For some, the early experience of animate nature was mysterious or even a little scary; for others it was simply a calm and quiet sense of being held by a presence, a personality cloaked in green leaves, clear flowing water, soft brown earth, moss and fern. As children, we experience the Earth as alive.

But how quickly we forget. Or rather, how quickly we are initiated and indoctrinated into the cult of reductionism … as in, "the tree is *just* a tree", "the rock is *just* a rock", "the Earth is *just* earth". In the reductionist worldview of scientific materialism, it is imperative that the cosmos is stripped of every vestige of personality, agency, soul. And before a child is finished elementary school, she has been effectively robbed of a way of experiencing the natural world which is immediate, imaginal, and utterly relational. By high school at latest, living nature has been transformed into mindless matter, a resource waiting to be exploited for human gain.

So is there a way back (or forward) into Eden? Is there a path we can take which will lead us deep into the primordial forest, where we can rediscover our original connection to all the wonderful creatures with whom we share this planet? So many of us are haunted by a collective memory of the Dream Time, the days of the First Parents, when Eve and Adam could talk to the animals and understand the languages of all the plants and trees, when the wind told us secrets, and the water sang melodies which were already ancient by the time humans arrived on the scene. Are these days utterly lost to us? Or is there a way to reconnect to "all our relations", to our cousins in the animal, plant, and mineral realms?

Ironically, on a personal level, it might be easier for me to find such a pathway were I not a Christian. If I was a Wiccan or a Taoist or a traditional Cree, I would be immersed in a worldview and a set of spiritual practices designed to facilitate and enhance my relationship with the living Earth and the spirits of nature which surround us. As a practising Pagan, I would have access to teachings and psycho-spiritual technologies which would help me find my place, once again, in the web of energy and consciousness which permeates the entire universe.

As a Christian, however, I find that these life-ways have been all but cut off from me. Now don't misunderstand – there are many good things about the Christian faith, and many reasons why I remain a convinced and convicted believer in the Way of Christ Jesus. But let's face it, in the contemporary mainstream churches of modern western society, we no longer have a functional spiritual cosmology. We have all kinds of engaging theologies – that is, words about God – but nothing that serves us well as a map of the spirit world. North American and western European culture is dominated by the presuppositions of scientific materialism, and the church has imbibed this reductionist worldview as if it were gospel truth. We've found ways to smuggle in God and the human soul, but anything "spiritual" beyond that is pretty much treated with scorn and intellectual contempt.

Surveying the long history of Christian thought and practice, we find of course that it wasn't always so. There were exceptions and marginal traditions which opened doors for Christians to step out onto the green paths. Early

Celtic forms of Christianity were one such example; the Spirit-drenched *viriditas* of Hildegard was another. Francis of Assisi, in his own unique way, invited the church to pay closer attention to the rest of creation, and there are others who have followed in his footsteps. But these brilliant examples of "green faith" seem to be exceptions to the normative path of ignoring, or even denigrating, the non-human world.

I expect that this present work will be met in many quarters by incredulity and open hostility. "Christian animism", for many, can suggest nothing more than crude syncretism, a blasphemous oxymoron. I hope to challenge that view, though my intention is more apologetic than polemic. I write from my own experience, and I draw on the experiences and reflections of many who find themselves on the fringes of church and society. I pay attention to Witches, Buddhists, faery-watchers, deep ecologists, and Elders. I also search out the fertile places of my own tradition, seeking to hear a Word of healing for our Earth, a Word of grace for the trees and the animals, a Word of invitation back to the garden of Creation, our once and future home.

For those who are interested to know such things, I want to acknowledge the work of two primary guides in my intellectual formation of Christian animism: Walter Wink and Starhawk. Wink, in his masterful trilogy on the Powers, introduced me to the biblical category of the "angels of nature", and provided a conceptual framework which made sense of the relationship between spirit and matter, heavenly and earthly. Starhawk challenged me to keep moving from the head to the heart, from "talking self" to "younger self", from theory to practice. Thinking about the spirits of land and woods is one thing; encountering them, communicating with them, ministering to them, is quite another. Starhawk and Wink both held up a warning as well: the work we do with the multiplicity of beings in creation is never simply personal; it is simultaneously political. Mere sentimentalism is blind to the real powers at work in the destruction of the Earth and **all** her children, and gives us no tools to resist the war-makers, strip-miners, clear-cutters, and polluters around us and within us. A truly green spirituality will engage us in the work of Earth-protection and Earth-healing, in many forms and venues. It is my hope that these reflections on Christian animism will make at least a small contribution to that larger work of which we are all a part.

Part 1: Introducing Christian Animism

Definitions

So what exactly is "Christian animism"? It's a valid question, as these two words are rarely held together, and more often placed in stark opposition to each other. It may be helpful to begin with a working definition of the term "animism". The Shorter Oxford claims that animism is "the attribution of a living soul to inanimate objects and natural phenomena." The term emerged during the early stages of nineteenth-century cultural anthropology, as a way to describe "primitive" peoples' understanding of religion. In many ways, it was a subtly derogatory term, implicitly suggesting that animism was a stage in the evolution of religion, which would "grow up" into polytheism, then henotheism, and finally culminate in a "mature" monotheism. There are other problems with the term as well, one of which is the misunderstanding that animism describes essentially "disembodied" spirits which inhabit or possess otherwise "inanimate" things, such as rocks or trees. This view is a product of a mechanistic and dualistic understanding of the universe, and as such distorts the actual beliefs and practices of the various animist traditions in question.

Furthermore, animism is often confused with other concepts such as ancestral reverence and polytheism. Certainly, all of these phenomena are related to each other, and often co-exist in a given religious worldview; in this work however, we will concentrate primarily on the nature spirits, or "spirits of the land".

These weaknesses aside, I still find that animism is a useful term. Set in the context of a worldview which sees spirit as the "interiority" of matter, rather than its dualistic opposite, animism can be reclaimed as a concept which sees the natural world as sentient, personable, and very much alive. It helps us to experience and understand each created entity, from a prairie gopher to a Rocky Mountain range, as a *person*, someone to whom we are related. That is basically what I mean when I use the word animism. Later in this essay I will develop more fully the cosmological worldview which enables and supports this type of under-standing.

Christian animism, then, is simply what happens when a committed Christian engages the world and each creature as alive, sentient, and related, rather than soul-less and ontologically inferior. However, that's not really "simple", is it? This type of stance vis-à-vis the natural world would have enormous implications for **all** aspects of Christian belief and practice. What would liturgy look like, for instance, if we knew that plants, animals, and whole ecosystems were co-worshippers with us? How would our eschatologies change if we had to "make room" in heaven for the entire created order? Would our ethical processes morph if "love your neighbour" now included cows, plankton, and all manner of creepy-crawlies? And what does pastoral care look like for trees anyways? All of these, and more, are questions with which a Christian animist perspective must engage.

A few words are in order at this point about the relationship between Christian animism and various forms of theological cosmology. It is very easy to get these things mixed up: I consider Christian animism to be a type of *spiritual* cosmology (dealing with the nature of the spirit world, and all its various entities), whereas *theological* cosmology deals with the relationship between God and the universe. Of course, the two categories overlap, but it is important to note the difference. Many contemporary theologians are doing very good work in the area of theological cosmology, critiquing traditional forms of supernatural theism (which stresses the utter transcendence of God), and moving toward more of a trinitarian panentheism (a worldview which seeks a balance between divine immanence and transcendence, asserting that all things are in God and God is in all things). Sally McFague's model of the universe as the body of God is a prime example of this type of theological cosmology. This is good work and reflection that is extremely necessary for the church as we move into an ecological age, where our models of the God-world relationship must be able to uphold an eco-friendly praxis. But still, this is not the same as spiritual cosmology. In fact, throughout much of Christian history, various forms of theological cosmology and their attendant practices of piety and mysticism have functioned to subsume actual created entities into the human quest for God. In other words, even "Earth-friendly" forms of Christianity such as Franciscan spirituality or Meister Eckhart's Rhine Valley mysticism, have tended to see other created beings as a means to an end. Nature is contemplated in order to lead us to God, rather than to engage in relationship-building with our non-human neighbours. We have inherited from our neo-platonic heritage a distinct prejudice against "the many" in favour of "the One".

A spiritual cosmology such as Christian animism helps us to experience, understand, and relate to "the many" – that is, the actual created beings which constitute the universe. My sense is that while panentheism is the natural ally of Christian animism, it is not impossible to embrace Christian animism as a classical theist, or even as a pantheist or atheist (although there may be considerably more discussion about whether these worldviews are compatible with Christianity). The point is that Christian animism recognizes that there is ultimately more to our faith than God and the human soul. Christian animism is a perspective and a path that allows us to navigate the spirit world, the "interiority" and energy of Indra's Net, the vast web of beings with whom we share this fragile Earth, our island home, and to whom we are intimately related.

Oppositions

Frankly, however, not everyone is going to be convinced. I know that there will always be those who believe that Christianity and animism are utterly incompatible. Since people rarely shift worldviews through argument, I am not going to spill a lot of ink trying to convince anyone who does not want to be convinced. On the other hand, it is important to engage at some level with those who are opposed to the idea of Christian animism. The objections come primarily from two different perspectives: the scientific and the theological.

Many modern western people can relate to the poster which Agent Molder has hanging on the wall in his small dingy office in the popular '90s TV show, *The X-Files*. The poster shows a UFO in flight, and contains the caption "I want to believe..." The problem is that the worldview into which we are sold has no room whatsoever for belief. It only has room for scientifically verifiable "knowledge". This is not a diatribe against science per se, but rather an acknowledgment that the reductionist model of scientific materialism is an ideology which has captured the collective imagination of the west, and will not allow us to believe in that which cannot be quantified. "Religious" people can sometimes manage to get some sort of "exemption" for God and the human soul, but then to relate these amorphous entities to the actual physical universe becomes a bit of a stretch, to say the least. Religion is reduced to the production of meaning, rather than the facilitation of a bodily encounter with the Living God and Her world full of wonderful creatures.

It seems to me that the Newtonian model of the universe is entirely adequate for the tasks of architectural design, billiards, and the like, but when it begins to function as an epistemological ideology, policing the borders of what we can know, it oversteps its bounds. While objectivity may be a laudable goal within scientific research, there comes a point when "objectivism" becomes an idol. There is no such thing as "value-free" science, even less so the more scientific research is hijacked by globalized industry.

The problem is not science, nor even scientific materialism. The problem is a phenomenon called reductionism – a philosophical tendency to subdivide an entity into its smallest components, cut it off from its inherent relation to a larger context, and "reduce" it to a quantifiable analysis. Whenever you hear yourself or someone else say "well, it's just some bad pizza I ate last night", or "it's just the wind in the trees", or "don't worry, it's just hormones", you are dealing with reductionism on its popular level. Whenever we seek to provide simple analysis of complex phenomena, we run the risk of falling into reductionism.

When it comes to our relationship with the world of nature, reductionism teams up with scientific materialism and industrial pragmatism to create a deadly ideology which not only cuts us off from any meaningful form of communion with the non-human world, but also sets the stage for a full-scale blitzkrieg of exploitation of "natural resources". In *Unmasking the Powers*, Walter Wink observes that:

the idea of living matter was simply economically inconvenient. In the participative worldview of Medieval Europe, one could certainly mine nature's ores, but only with care and devotion. Metallurgy was deliberately compared to obstetrics, and new mines were sunk, until the fifteenth century, accompanied by religious ceremonies in which the miners fasted, prayed, and observed a particular series of rites. But if nature is dead, then there are no restraints on exploiting it for profits (155).

The contribution of scientific materialism to ecological biocide is staggering and profound. This connection alone should make us step back and re-evaluate the prominence we give to science in determining our worldview. It is important to note that some of the strongest critiques of materialist reductionism are coming from within the scientific community itself: quantum mechanics, chaos theory, ecology – each of these disciplines are recognizing the limits of the Newtonian model for observing and describing reality. As theologians rediscover the word "energy" as a synonym for "spirit", scientists are simultaneously developing an openness to questions almost religious in nature. Is the war between religion and science coming to an end? Well, that might be a bit optimistic, but at least there are, here and there, small signs of ceasefire.

Of course, I am quite aware that none of this will change the mind of anyone ideologically committed to a worldview based on scientific reductionism. But for those who, like Agent Molder, "want to believe", I would simply suggest that belief is possible. Scientific scepticism need not cut us off completely from the chance to experience the world around us as alive, sentient, and "personable". In fact, a healthy dose of scepticism is absolutely necessary in all forms of spiritual exploration; let's just remember to be sceptical about our scepticism as well!

The other main source of objection to the idea of Christian animism comes, not surprisingly, from the theological perspective. Christianity does not have a great track record when it comes to making room for dialogue with animist positions, and there are many reasons for this. My sense is that the root cause however has been a confusion in the relationship between animism, pantheism, and polytheism. This is not surprising, since in many of the cultures which Christianity has encountered, these three categories have been functionally interchangeable.

Let's define the terms as simply as possible. Animism is a belief that non-human creatures are alive, sentient, and "personable". Pantheism is the belief that God is the totality of all things, and that all things are God. Polytheism is the belief that there are many gods to be worshipped. Although each of these terms has a distinct meaning, in practice they have tended to overlap. So in any given pagan culture, there is a sophisticated and complex pattern of religious thinking that recognizes divinity spread throughout the universe. Divinity wears many "masks" and manifests itself in a multitude of gods and goddesses. These deities are to be respected and related to in various ways, and often worship or reverence is directed toward the deity through a living being such as a tree, or through a totem animal, or through an "inanimate" (by some definitions) entity such as a rock or a spring of water. Although this is a generalization, and the actual religious matrix would vary from culture to culture, we can see how the three categories of pantheism, polytheism, and animism overlap.

For Christians, it has been extremely difficult to tell the difference between these strands of thought; in fact, the church has been polemically conditioned to *not* see the difference. With unrelenting consistency, early Christian teachers employed the strategy, inherited from Jewish monotheism as well as Greek philosophy, of labelling any form of relation to a spiritual entity (other than God or an angel) as superstitious, idolatrous, or demonic. Pantheism, polytheism, and animism were three aspects of the same religious paradigm, and it was a paradigm attacked mercilessly by the church, sometimes with very little comprehension of the complexity of the religion involved.

While in no way trying to justify the religious bigotry and imperialistic violence unleashed by the church on pagan cultures throughout the Constantinian era (that is, from the fourth century CE to the present), I can understand why Christians have been wary of pantheism and polytheism (although there could have been other ways to interpret these categories more respectfully than the typical crude polemic against idolatry and demon-worship). But it seems to me that animism, separated from the other two strands of the paradigm, does not in and of itself pose a problem to basic Christian convictions. Let's take an example: the apple tree in my backyard. I believe this tree is alive, that it is conscious and sentient, and that I can relate to it, in some sense, as a "person". I can commune and even communicate with it. I believe it to be a fellow creature, a being both physical and spiritual, as I am. But I don't worship it, and I don't consider it a god. It is simply a neighbour. Now, while you may think me a bit off my rocker for holding this belief, you cannot accuse me of being a heretic. And in fact, this perspective on the world may be even more "biblical" than our modern scientific worldviews. The psalms are filled with references to the created world being alive and sentient, full of praise for the Creator. It is we who are deaf, not the world which is mute!

At some deep level, we know this to be true. In fact, I believe that one of the reasons why Tolkien's *Middle Earth* and Lewis' *Narnia* have been so wildly popular is that they both present fictionalized and narrative examples of Christian animism. Both worlds contain a multitude of beings, including elves, dwarves, talking trees, water spirits, river gods, talking animals, and a host of other creatures, each of whom breaks down our simplistic categories of "person" and "nature".

Ultimately, there need be no theological objections to Christian animism. It is no more pantheistic nor polytheistic than the Bible itself. Christian animism certainly accords to the non-human creation much more sentience, agency, and "soul" than has typically been the case within the Christian tradition, but it is well within the boundaries of doctrinal orthodoxy. More than that, Christian animism can even contribute to the authentic development of orthodoxy, as the church grows into the ecological challenges of a new millennium.

Implications

So what do we gain by adopting for ourselves the worldview of Christian animism? Does it further the mission of the church? Does it intensify our quest for justice? Does it deepen our spiritual discipleship? Or does it simply open us to fear and scorn from within our own tradition?

Christian animism, as perspective and practice, has many implications for the future of the church. There are three areas in particular which deserve attention as foci for discussion of the benefits of Christian animism: ecology, inter-faith dialogue, and personal spirituality. In each of these areas, Christian animism opens doors for the church which have been tightly closed in the past.

Ecology is probably the most obvious field engaged by a Christian animist perspective. It may also be the most important as well, since the church seems to have precious few conceptual and practical resources when it comes to relating responsibly to the rest of creation. We have seen the damage caused by a long-term commitment to the "human-dominion" model, especially coupled with modern utilitarian versions of corporate control. The contemporary Christian shift to "stewardship" as our preferred means of relating to the Earth is only marginally better, a sort of soft-core dominion approach, which still privileges the human species above all others as chosen and competent to make wise and just decisions about the "use" of "natural resources". Both dominion and stewardship models are rigorously anthropocentric, leading many ecological philosophers to question the ability of Christianity to become Earth-friendly. In *Ecology and Religion*, David Kinsley asserts that:

> the critique of the Bible and Christianity as constituting primarily negative influences in the advent and development of contemporary ecological crises usually makes three general arguments to support its point of view. First, in the Bible and Christianity nature is stripped of its gods, goddesses, and spirits and ceases to be regarded as divine. Second, the Bible and Christianity are strongly anthropocentric and teach that human beings are divinely ordained to rule over and dominate all other species and nature generally. Third, many Christian writings, and much Christian theology, relegates nature and matter generally to a low status relative to the divine, which is equated with spirit alone (103).

There are many contemporary theologians and practitioners working hard to rectify some of these ecological shortfalls in the faith. Ecological, eco-feminist, process, creation-centred, and green-liberation theologies (as well as the more evangelical "creation care" movement) have all begun to challenge the status quo of "toxic" Christianity. Individual believers are also finding ways of "greening" their faith, sometimes even blending Christianity with other religious perspectives such as Buddhism, Wicca, or traditional Indigenous spirituality.

Christian animism adds another perspective and set of practices for the ecologically-minded believer. It has the added bonus of engaging ecologically with the world by forming direct relationships with the actual created beings who surround us on a daily basis: our animal companions and houseplants, the trees on the block, the local watershed, birds and animals in the park or woods nearby. Sustained and energized by a network of real neighbours in the natural world, our ecological disciplines become less abstract, less duty-driven, and much more personal, concrete, and even fun!

Closely related to the subject of ecology is that of interfaith dialogue. It is a well-known fact that we live today in a pluralistic society, and that for this society to become peaceful, just, and ecologically sustainable, we will all have to find ways of working together. Christians, on this front, have much to learn from the "green" religions – that is, those faiths which have not cut themselves off from the natural world in favour of an exclusively anthropocentric soteriology. Christian animism can go a long way toward building a sense of "common ground" with these religious perspectives. Although we may have different ideas about God/dess, there can at least be a shared experience of relating to the natural world as alive, sentient, and personable. In the next chapter, we will spend considerable time looking at several examples of "green" religious traditions, with special focus on how each of them "do" animism in their own context. Learning in this manner, from other religions rather than directly from our own tradition, is a good skill to have when it comes to fruitful inter-faith dialogue. It is something we seldom do, but could benefit from immensely.

Finally, it is my hope that Christian animism will help Christian believers deepen their own faith and spirituality. So much of our piety is focussed on "heaven", or on the human community of the church, that we miss out on developing real relationships with the rest of creation. Christian animism can give us some tools so that we might begin to open our hearts and minds to the "spirit world", not as a realm far removed from day-to-day reality, and not as a synonym for heaven (as an eschatological reality), but rather as the world of energy and consciousness intricately bound to the physical creatures whom we encounter in our real lives. It is the world of interiority, accessed through our own interior imaginal (not imaginary!) sensibilities, as well as our physical senses. Christian animism helps us engage the depth dimension of the world around us, and in doing so, opens up incredible realities and vistas of spiritual "terrain" which have been largely inaccessible to us in the past.

Part 2: Learning from Others

Sadly to say, my own journey of personal exploration into the world of animism has rarely been nurtured or supported by my own faith tradition of Christianity. I have been a Christian for over 25 years and a priest for more than a decade. In all that time, I can count on both hands the number of Christians I have met (in person or in print) who strive to embody the type of spiritual cosmology I am describing as Christian animism. This is not to deny or minimize the tremendous work being done by scholars and practitioners to advance ecological forms of theology and praxis, but rarely does this work extend to practical models of relating to other creatures as neighbours and friends. No one has taught me, as a Christian, how to talk to the trees, how to worship with animals, how to heal the land. For these teachings, I have found myself drawn to the insights and wisdom of the Pagan world. (I hope the reader will recognize by now that I use the word "Pagan", like the term "animism", with much respect, and stripped of its derogatory connotations.)

For years I have struggled to reconcile my "inner Pagan" with the faith of Jesus, whom I so dearly love. It is only as I slowly come out of the "broom closet", and accept my own Pagan inclinations as a God-given gift, that I can acknowledge the gratitude I feel towards those of other religious traditions who have taught me so much. Were it not for the writings and public teachings of Witches, Buddhists, Aboriginal Elders, and various Neo-Pagans, I would not have reached the point of articulating the tentative Christian animism which has become my own spirituality.

The rest of this section is devoted to a summary of five

sources of religious tradition which have impacted me most deeply. In exploring these traditions, I will be paying close attention to the specifically animist aspects of the religion, rather than attempting to describe in detail the whole framework of the faith. Also, I will be "reading" the traditions, interpreting them, through Christian eyes, asking as a Christian what each tradition has to teach Christianity.

Of the five religious perspectives, the first three (Neo-Paganism, Engaged Buddhism, and Cree Traditions) are not my own in any significant way. The last two (Enochian Apocalypticism and Celtic Christianity) are much closer to my own religious stream, but far away from me in terms of history (second century BCE and fifth—seventh centuries CE, respectively). An exploration of each of these traditions should help the reader get a clearer sense of what an animistic perspective entails, and how this perspective can inform a green and vibrant Christian piety.

Neo-Paganism

In many ways it is difficult to articulate a working defin-ition of Neo-Paganism as the phenomenon is intrinsically polymorphous and, well, new. Jesse Wolf Hardin, renowned "Gain Wizard", calls Neo-Paganism New Nature Spirituality, and describes it as follows:

New Nature Spirituality incorporates or is resonant and allied with various aspects of ancient primal mind, Shamanism, Totemism, Animism, Paganism, Buddhism, Norse Cosmology, the Animism of Africa, the "Red Road" of Native America, Celtic Druidry, and archaic Wicca. And yet it is more than a re-enactment or resur-facing of earlier traditions, more than a return to the "old ways". Included within are elements of contemporary theosophy, ecospirituality, ecofeminism, Unitarianism, communitarianism, creation spirituality, deep ecology, conservation biology, ecopsychology, and new science. We're not talking about an amalgam of favourite ideas, so much as directly accessing the same inspirited Source that has informed every magical practice throughout time: the living world, Gaia! (*Gaia Eros*, 22)

It is scarcely possible to comprehend the essence of Neo-Paganism in its myriad forms without understanding this sense of total respect for the planet. In Christianity, while we confess that the Earth is a good creation of a good Creator, our dominant forms of theology give no indication that this planet is intrinsically sacred and revelatory. For the Neo-Pagan on the other hand, divinity is not envisioned as in any way separate, or transcendent, in relation to the Earth (who is often called Gaia or Mother or Goddess). Starhawk, one of the most popular and important teachers in the Wiccan movement, gives a helpful description of the relationship between divinity and nature for Neo-Pagans:

People often ask me if I *believe* in the Goddess. I reply, 'Do you believe in rocks?' It is extremely difficult for most Westerners to grasp the concept of a manifest deity. The phrase 'believe *in*' itself implies that we cannot *know* the Goddess, that She is somehow intangible, incomprehensible. But we do not *believe* in rocks – we may see them, touch them, dig them out of our gardens, or stop small children from throwing them at each other. We know them; we connect with them. In the Craft, we do not *believe* in the Goddess – we connect with Her; through the moon, the stars, the ocean, the earth, through trees, animals, through other human beings, through ourselves. She is here. She is within us all. She is the full circle: earth, air, fire, water, and essence – body, mind, spirit, emotions, change (*The Spiral Dance*, 91-92).

For Neo-Pagans, the fact that divinity is utterly immanent means that each and every creature has something to teach us. And not just in a metaphorical way, as an analogy for a spiritual principle or a face of God/dess. Each creature can also teach us about itself, and reveal its inner life to us. A tree spirit can tell us what it needs at any given time, it can tell us stories of the forest's history; it can raise its voice in worship and add its own unique strength to our prayers and our actions for the good of the life-community.

A very good example of this type of inter-species communication is the work of the Findhorn Community in Scotland. In the mid-1960s, a small spiritual family set up a caravan trailer on a sandy plot of land near Findhorn village. Through years of faithful meditation and loving attention to the spirits of the place, members of the community were able to communicate with the devas (or angels/spirits) of the small garden they planted. In turn, these devas cooperated with the humans, and through this creative synergy the once infertile plot of wind-buffeted sand and gravel was transformed into a patch of paradise. Huge vegetables were growing in the garden which boggled the minds of scientists and spiritualists alike. One of the co-founders of the Findhorn Community, a Canadian named Dorothy Maclean, was given direction by God through an astonishing piece of guidance. These are the words she heard:

Yes, you are to cooperate in the garden. Begin this by thinking about the nature spirits, the higher over lighting nature spirits, and tune into them. That will be so unusual as to draw their interest here. They will be overjoyed to find some members of the human race eager for their help. That is the first step. By the higher nature spirits, I mean those such as the spirits of clouds, of rain, and of vegetables. The smaller individual nature spirits are under their jurisdiction. In the new world these realms will be quite open to humans – or should I say, humans will be open to them. Seek into the glorious realms of nature with sympathy and understanding, knowing that these beings are of the Light, willing to help, but suspicious of humans and on the lookout for the false, the snags. Keep with Me and they will find none, and you will all build toward the new (*The Findhorn Garden*, 57).

Though Findhorners may self-identify more as new-agers than Neo-Pagans, their distinct variety of animistic practice has been instrumental in demonstrating the Neo-Pagan goal of communion, communication, and cooperation with nature spirits. For many Neo-Pagans, these nature spirits are understood and envisioned as the faery-folk: elves, dwarves, gnomes, etc. Drawing on stories and imagery from classical and folk culture, the living world of nature is seen to be populated by an abundance of beings who are intimately connected with the life and health of the eco-region in which they dwell.

It is this deep connection with the inner life of natural entities that shapes both the spiritual and political praxis of committed Neo-Pagans of all stripes. If you ask a Witch about her piety or a Druid about his prayer life, you will hear an answer which draws your attention away from abstractions of creed and back down toward the embodied realities of Earth. Neo-Pagan spirituality, including the practice of magic, is focussed on fostering and enhancing deep connections with the land, with plants and animals, with the primal energies of the natural world. Therefore it comes as no surprise that various forms of ecological activism are the practical extension of Neo-Paganism's spiritual practice; indeed, most Neo-Pagans would not draw a line between their religious and ecological work. One flows naturally out of the other. In a worldview where divinity is embodied, service to the Goddess is service to the Earth and all her creatures.

For myself, the most compelling and engaging facet of Neo-Paganism is its ability to re-imagine the world as alive and full of magic. In some ways, it invites a mature return to the childhood world of the faery tale. This is not to denigrate or minimize the worldview in any way, but rather to celebrate its ability to open a doorway in the imagination to an Earth filled with wonder. And that is no small thing indeed.

Engaged Buddhism

A brief study of the early centuries of Buddhism and its missionary expansion throughout India, Southeast Asia, China, and Japan reveals a religion which (with notable exceptions) is much less explicitly political than the Abrahamic traditions of Judaism, Christianity, and Islam. With its focus on renunciation and its assessment of the world as *maya,* or illusion, Buddhism has not traditionally been seen as particularly political or activist in any modern sense of the term. However, since the 1960s, that assessment has begun to change; a transformation in Buddhism has been occurring, drawing monks and nuns out of the monasteries and into the streets, the soup kitchens, the prisons, and the war-zones of the world. The Vietnamese monk Thich Nhat Hanh was the first to use the term "engaged Buddhism" to describe this transformation, but others soon followed. In the East and in the West, Buddhists have become deeply involved in organizations and movements working for peace, justice, and the integrity of creation. Many profound teachers have emerged in North America, promoting this renewed form of Buddhism in the Western context.

For the purpose of the present study, I will focus on the teachings of engaged Buddhism which are particularly animistic. It is my understanding that as Buddhism spread through the East it tended to absorb the animist impulses of the indigenous peoples it encountered, such as the *Bon* shamanism of Tibet or the *Nat* devotion of Burma. But unlike Christianity, which generally suppressed animistic thought and practices in the people it evangelized, Buddhism already had a cosmological matrix which made room for sentience beyond the human species. It is the retrieval and creative reinterpretation of elements of this cosmology by theorists and practitioners of engaged Buddhism which is of primary interest for our study of animism.

In many ways, the foundation for engaged Buddhist animism and environmental activism is the *bodhisattvacarya*, a vow to help all living beings in the world. Stephanie Kaza notes that:

in the Mahayana tradition one takes up the bodhisattva path, vowing to return again and again to relieve the suffering of all sentient beings – the life work of an environmentalist! ... Budding eco-Buddhists struggle with the application of these spiritual vows in the very real contexts of factory farms, pesticide abuse, genetic engineering, and loss of endangered species habitat (*Engaged Buddhism in the West,* 168-69).

It is significant that the vow of service is not just toward suffering humanity, but to all living beings. While this is not animism per se, it certainly represents a precondition or predisposition toward animist sensibilities.

Another foundational aspect of engaged Buddhism is the image of the jewel net of Indra. Scholar and activist Joanna Macy describes Indra's net as:

a vision of reality structured very much like the holographic view of the universe, so that each being is at each node of the net, each jewel reflects all the others, reflecting back and catching the reflection, just as systems theory sees that the part contains the whole (*The Engaged Buddhist Reader,* 178).

From this perspective each entity of creation, not just the human, is present in all the others. The notion of the self therefore undergoes a radical transformation, whereby egocentricity becomes *eco*centricity, and the boundaries of the self "stretch" to include every living being. Again, while this is not specifically animist, it is a form of cosmology which makes animism more tenable as a stance within the world.

In 1988, New Society Publishers released an amazing book called *Thinking Like a Mountain: Toward a Council of All Beings.* The work was a collaboration of a number of key ecological philosophers, activists, and eco-Buddhists, including Joanna Macy, Gary Snyder, Pat Fleming, John Seed, and Arne Naess. What makes the book significant is that it is a collection of short meditative essays, poems, and practical exercises designed to help us enter imaginatively into the life-space and consciousness of other beings. In the introduction, John Seed describes the Council of All Beings as:

> a form of group work which prepares and allows people to 'hear within themselves the sounds of the earth crying', a phrase borrowed from Vietnamese Zen master Thich Nhat Hanh, and to let other life forms speak through them. It is a form which permits us to experience consciously the pain and the power of our interconnectedness with all life (7).

This type of ritual meditation draws on the Buddhist-influenced concept of the ecological self, as well as the model of interconnectedness suggested by Indra's net, taking theory into practice by teaching participants how to "feel into" the inner lives of other nonhuman beings. This cosmological openness within engaged Buddhism is a primary resource for us as we tentatively map out the contours of Christian animism.

Nehiyaw Tapsinawin (Cree Worldview)

> Indigenous cultures, while often quite different from one another, tend to emphasize gaining deep knowledge of and rapport with the land and the nonhuman beings that dwell within it ... For the most part, the land is affirmed to be alive, full of spirits and nonhuman creatures that have formed the land and continue to pervade it. To live in the land successfully, it is necessary to know and relate properly to these beings (David Kinsley in *Ecology and Religion*, 3).

Some time ago, I had an interesting conversation with a friend of mine, a Cree poet-priest. Beth and I were in seminary together, and we shared many thoughts with each other about the spiritual dynamics of First People – Newcomer relations. One of the things which stuck with me from a particular conversation was Beth's observation that newcomers (non-Indigenous people) would not truly find our place here in Turtle Island until we learned to engage with the spirits of the land. As I realized over time that she was not speaking metaphorically, I began to wonder how this "engagement" could occur, and what it would mean spiritually and theologically. In fact, it was this very conversation with Beth which crystallized my thoughts around Christian animism and led to the present study.

As an Anglican priest living in inner-city Saskatoon, Saskatchewan, I had been surrounded by Aboriginal neighbours. On my street and in my ministries I crossed paths with people of Cree, Saulteaux, Dene, Dakota, Lakota, Nakota, and Metis descent all the time. And yet, there is still such a cultural divide in our communities that it is hard to know if we will ever really live harmoniously. I don't know one Aboriginal family who hasn't been deeply affected by the residential school system, and other forms of colonial oppression. Imposed poverty, racism, and violence are ever-present factors in the lives of many of my Aboriginal neighbours. I name this reality as a form of confession: it is my own tradition which has been instrumental in the sustained colonial assault on Indigenous people over the past several centuries in this land. To be sure, Christianity is now embraced by many people of Aboriginal heritage as a vibrant and living faith, but that does not negate the shadow side of what my church has done in its perpetration of cultural genocide.

So what does all this have to do with animism? Well, to learn from a spiritual lineage which has been demonized by my own tradition, it is necessary for me to approach this tradition with much humility and in full awareness of broken treaties and broken relationships. I cannot come and plunder Nehiyaw spirituality in the same way that my people have plundered Cree land and resources. My own learning must be respectful, and needs to be accompanied by a commitment to give back to the culture, to work for a society where there is justice and restored harmony among the People. In addition to this, there is also a gnawing awareness on my part that the spirits of the land where I dwell may not be favourably disposed toward my people. They have seen what the newcomers have done, and I suspect they are not impressed. It is my theological conviction that the spirits of nature are children of the Creator, and faithful servants of the Cosmic Christ, but that doesn't necessarily mean that they are neutral in light of historical circumstances. Going back to Beth's observation, it may be that for me, as a white man and a priest of the "conquering" culture, I may have some work to do to rebuild trust before I can fruitfully engage with the spirits of this land. With that in mind, let us proceed with respect ...

In some ways it is difficult to say with complete precision which elements of Nehiyaw spiritual traditions are pre-contact, and which are borrowed from other Aboriginal traditions or from the Pan-Indian movement of the 1960s and 1970s. In any case, I will be paying attention to teachings that are found in contemporary Plains Cree culture.

One of the most basic and foundational of these teachings is the structure of the medicine wheel. The medicine wheel is a circle divided into four quarters; this basic form functions as a cosmological diagram, representing the circle of life, as well as the four elements, directions, races, stages of life, etc. As a symbol of diversity within unity, the medicine wheel makes visible the reality that all beings have a place within the circle of life, and that none are to be disregarded as inferior or of less importance. The smallest creature has wisdom to impart, and plays its own important role in the sacred whole. Balance and harmony, therefore, are primary virtues according to the medicine wheel teachings, and no part can inflate its sense of importance without damaging the whole. Many Cree stories illustrate this basic principle, often in humorous ways, as various characters (usually Wesakecak, the Trickster) upset the sacred balance, and then find ways to restore harmony.

Closely related to the circle of life teachings demonstrated by the medicine wheel is the basic conviction that much of the creation is animate (as witnessed by the language itself, where animate/inanimate replaces gender as a linguistic category). Non-human creatures are experienced as animate "people", with humans ("two-legged people") being one tribe among many others: the "four-legged people" (animals), the "winged people" (birds), the "finned people" (fish), and the "standing people" (plants). Rocks, waters, and even weather conditions are also considered alive and conscious in ways that western modernity considers quite foreign. In this context, hunting, gathering, and all elements of communal life are undertaken with extreme care and respect toward all the non-human peoples who support and uphold the lifeways of the human tribe. Communion and communication between species is accomplished through ritual and ceremony, and though the shaman or medicine person has primary responsibility in this type of exchange, cultivating relationship with otherkind is the normal way of being for each person, not just the religious specialist.

It is easy, however, to idealize and romanticize modern day Nehiyaw lifeways; the reality is that several centuries of colonialism have taken their toll. Much traditional knowledge has been lost due to the breaking of the generations during the residential school era. And now many of the Elders, who still know the old ways, are dying; at the same time, many of the youth are assimilated into urban contexts which place little value on ancient wisdom. When I asked my Cree language teacher if she thought that the knowledge would be lost forever with the passing of the Elders, she told me that the Elders themselves believe that ultimately the land holds the knowledge, and that the spirits will reveal through dream and vision the wisdom that is needed for the survival of the People. On a personal level, this is one of the reasons I am so concerned that we, as Christians, find ways to listen to the land and communicate with the spirits of nature. Christian animism can contribute a perspective and a set of practices to the church which will be very useful as we renew the spiritual treaties between Aboriginal and non-Aboriginal people, and work together to rebuild our communities and heal the Earth. In this way, Christ will again become good medicine for all the beings of Turtle Island.

Enochian Apocalypticism

Upon hearing the word "apocalyptic", the reader's mind is often consumed with images of bloodshed, destruction, horrible beasts, and the wrathful judgements of God. Furthermore, many people are exposed to apocalyptic literature through the fiery preaching of televangelists who make the most of its frightening elements in order to bully their audiences toward conversion. While it is true that biblical books such as Daniel and Revelation do contain images of doom and destruction, they are also the books most explicitly cosmological in nature; that is, they are filled with reflections on the structure and destiny of the created order. The word apocalypse means "revealing" or "unveiling", and apocalyptic literature functions to describe mysteries or secrets which have been hidden since "the foundations of the world". Apocalypse points us toward "things above (heaven), things below (hell or the underworld), things before (the creation of the world), and things to come (the judgement and consummation of the world)".

The apocalyptic books of the Bible with which we are familiar have their roots in an older layer of textual tradition often called the Enoch corpus, of which 1 (or Ethiopian) Enoch is most well known. 1 Enoch is a collection of apocalyptic texts which most scholars believe was were composed between the fourth century BCE and the turn of the era (Nickelsburg & Vaderkam, vii), though at least one scholar (Margaret Barker) asserts that fragments of these texts belong to the priesthood of the First Temple period.

For present purposes, we are concerned with the elements of this Enochian tradition which hint at a much more animistic worldview than is usually presented by the Bible (discounting of course the Book of Psalms, which is thoroughly animistic). One of the main characteristics of Enochian lore is its preoccupation with the realm of angels. In the apocalyptic worldview, the whole cosmos is permeated by angelic presence. Whereas we might be inclined to view angels as residing "'round the heavenly throne", and making the occasional visit to earth to convey some divine message, the Enochian literature is much more bold in imagining a multiplicity of roles for angelic (and demonic) beings throughout the whole creation. In this body of work, Enoch speaks of the spirits of the thunder, the sea, the hoar frost, the hail, the mist, the dew, and the rain (1 Enoch 60:15-22, 61:10). There is also mention made of angels of seasons, years, rivers, seas, fruit, grass, and everything bubbling (2 Enoch 19:1-6). The Book of Jubilees, a related text, speaks as well of the creation of all the spirits which God created on the first day, including "the angels of the spirits of cold and of heat, and of winter and of spring and of autumn and of summer, and of all the spirits of God's creatures which are in the heavens and on the earth" (Jubilees 2:2).

In short, the Enochian lore reveals a universe in which all created beings have a spiritual aspect. While much of this literature is considered pseudopigraphical and non-canonical, the worldview it presents contributes to the ease with which the Book of Psalms speaks of created beings other than humans singing praise to God, and serving God with faithfulness. Though we have been taught to read these psalms as metaphorical, it would be wise to revisit this assumption. Through the visionary eyes of Enoch, we catch a glimpse of a universe filled with the glory of God, a world where each created being is in some respect angelic, a spirit created for praise and faithful service in the kin-dom of Love.

Celtic Christianity

Since my pilgrimage to the British Isles, and my sojourn on the blessed Isle of Iona more than two decades ago, I have become more and more convinced that there are treasures of wisdom and power in the early Celtic tradition which could be tremendous gifts for our churches today. Though it is always easy to romanticize the Celtic "golden age" (the early fifth to eighth centuries in the Celtic countries of Ireland, Scotland, Wales, and parts of northern England), the truth of the matter is that this tradition gives us one of the only examples we have of a relatively harmonious blending of Christian and pre-Christian ways in a truly indigenous church. For this reason, the study and retrieval of Celtic Christianity is foundational for the creation of a Christian animism suitable for modern western believers. And on a personal level, this is where my own ancestral roots are.

One of the most engaging facets of Celtic Christianity is its hagiography (stories of the saints). The most well-known saint is of course St. Patrick, but there are other holy characters in the fold of the Celtic churches which are also worth investigating: St. Brigit, St. Columba, St. David, and many others. The stories of the saints are permeated by the dramatic rural settings in which they lived, and even the asceticism of the monks and nuns is tempered by an irresistible love of nature. In her book *A World Made Whole*, Esther De Wall reports of these holy ones that:

> their lives became intertwined with the times and colours and rhythms of the world around them. They read the psalms and said the hours in peace with the birds. They lived close to the sound of the wind in the trees, the changing light of night and day, the cries of the birds. They ate berries, nuts and herbs, and drank water from the spring. It was a life of renunciation and yet a life that was totally fulfilled (71).

A recurrent theme in the stories of the saints is their relationship with particular animals. St. Kevin, for example, was said to have been at prayer one day, with his arms outstretched, when a blackbird settled in his hand and laid her eggs. Rather than disturb their nesting place, Kevin remained in that posture until the young birds were fully hatched. St. Columbanus, who taught the precept:

> "if you want to know the Creator, understand created things", would "call the beasts and the birds to him as he walked, and they would come straightaway, rejoicing and gambolling around him in great delight … He would summon a squirrel from the tree tops and let it climb all over him, and from time to time its head might be seen peeping through the folds of his robes" (De Waal, 82).

Likewise, St. Cuthbert, after a night of prayer in the beach-waters of Lindisfarne, was blessed with the companionship of two small sea-otters who would warm his frozen legs and dry them with their fur.

For the Celts, who never fully repudiated the traditions and worldview inherited from their pre-Christian ancestors, these stories were an expression of a healthy relationship between humans and animals. Wild creatures, in a very real sense, were seen to be "people": sentient beings with personality, compassion, and a capacity for holiness. The ability of the saints to cultivate such interesting relationships with animals was seen to be a sign of their growing sanctity. The logic behind this was that as a person came closer to God, she or he would also regain gifts from the Edenic world before the fall, one of which was the ability to communicate with the animals in a manner similar to that of Adam and Eve. Unlike many other Christian traditions which stressed a detachment from creation in the pursuit of Heaven, the Celtic path assumed that the heavenly calling would produce a more vibrant relationship with the creatures of Earth.

This emphasis on the goodness of the natural world can also be seen in the visual art of the period. Celtic manuscripts such as the *Book of Kells* are filled with ornate whorls and patterns of knotwork interwoven with animals, fish, birds, humans, and semi-divine creatures, held in dynamic tension with the biblical text itself. Many of the huge stone crosses dotting the Irish landscape feature scriptural and monastic motifs combined with striking images from the world of nature. Indeed, the distinctive form of the Celtic cross itself can be interpreted as the circle of creation and the cross of redemption fused in grace.

This interweaving of the natural, divine, and human worlds represents a general proclivity within Celtic Christianity to assimilate or "baptize" key elements of the older indigenous worldview into the new faith, in a manner almost wholly unique in the ancient Christian world. That is not to say that the early monks and missionaries didn't challenge aspects of the Druidic faith and Celtic culture, but by and large there seemed to be much more continuity between the old faith and the new. Taliesin, the sixth-century Welsh bard, proclaimed that:

> Christ the Word was from the beginning our Teacher, and we never lost his teachings. Christianity was in Asia a new thing, but there was never a time when the Druids of Britain held not its doctrines.

Well, this may be a bit of a stretch, but Taliesin's sentiments were indicative of the trend to affirm rather than reject the religious culture and traditions of his people. In fact, one of the titles which St. Columba bestows on Christ is "my Chief Druid", and Columba himself went for an extended period of study with the bard Gemman, a keeper of the pre-

Christian tales and songs. Ian Bradley, in *The Celtic Way*, states that:

> in many ways this approach comes close to what would nowadays be called syncretism. It did not involve a wholesale acceptance of pagan influences and practices and a blurring of all distinctions between different religions but it was naturally inclusive and synthetic in spirit, seeking always to incorporate and accommodate different perspectives within the universal embrace of Christ (94).

Perhaps the most well-known expression of the Celtic tendency toward an animistic worldview can be seen in this verse of "St. Patrick's Breastplate":

I arise today
Through a mighty strength, the invocation of the Trinity,
Through belief in the threeness,
Through confession of the oneness
Of the Creator of Creation.
I arise today
Through the strength of heaven:
Light of sun
Radiance of moon,
Splendour of fire,
Speed of lightning,
Swiftness of wind,
Depth of sea,
Stability of earth,
Firmness of rock.

For the ancient Celt, Christian or Pagan, the world around them was alive, its elements full of power, its creatures eager for communication and ready to help. Had it only been the early Celts who had met the First Peoples of Turtle Island, our shared history might have been quite different, and much happier. One can hope and pray that it is never too late for healing.

In this section we have looked at several forms of animistic thought and practice from which we can learn as we seek to articulate a specifically Christian animism. Learning from others, be they Neo-Pagan, engaged Buddhist, Nehiyaw (Cree), Enochian, or Celtic, is an important first step; inter-faith listening, across cultures or across time periods, can be a challenge, but it is well worth the effort. As we turn now to the construction of a Christian animist worldview, we do so with the insight and inspiration gained from careful listening to others.

Part 3: Spirits of the Land

An Integral Worldview

To say that a Christian can, and should, cultivate a relationship with the spirits of nature, the spirits of the land, is something new. What was natural and somewhat unconscious up until the end of the medieval period now requires consciousness and intentionality. To develop this relationship requires a conceptual framework which can assist our understanding of what the spirits of the land, of plants, of animals, of weather conditions, actually are.

Christian animism entails a profound shift in worldview. As stated previously, Christian animism does not require a rethinking of God (theology) so much as it does a revisioning of the universe (cosmology). For those of us trained in modern western habits of thought, it is a far stretch to imagine a world which is filled with sentience and "personality" beyond human individuals. Part of the reason for this is to be found in the long history of operative paradigms in western intellectual history. Biblical scholar Walter Wink, in his stellar trilogy on the powers and principalities, describes the progression of worldviews which have got us where we are. The following discussion is heavily indebted to Wink's proposals.

For Wink, the angels (or spirits) of nature are considered to be a subcategory of a wider phenomenon called "principalities and powers". For many, this phrase conjures up images of demons and wholly negative forces in life, but Wink maintains that the term in itself is neutral, and can refer to both angelic and demonic beings. It is worth quoting him extensively for a more detailed description of these entities:

> The Powers, unfortunately, have long since been identified as an order of angelic beings in heaven, or as demons flapping about in the sky. Most people have simply consigned them to the dustbin of superstition. Others, sensing the tremendous potential in the concept of the Powers for interpreting social reality, have identified them without remainder as institutions, structures, and systems. The powers certainly are the latter, but they are more, and it is that "more" that holds the clue to their profundity. In the biblical view they are both visible *and* invisible, earthly *and* heavenly, spiritual *and* institutional. ... The Powers are the simultaneity of an outer, visible structure and an inner, spiritual reality. The Powers, properly speaking, are not just the spirituality of institutions, but their outer manifestations as well. ... It is the spiritual aspect, however, that is so hard for people inured to materialism to grasp (*Engaging the Powers*, 3).

In his writing Wink is focusing here on the powers of the social, political, and economic aspects of our world, but he applies a similar framework to the powers of nature, seeing plants, animals, weather patterns, and ecosystems – indeed, all created beings – as having both material and spiritual aspects. To further explain this framework, Wink describes four distinct paradigms which have functioned previously in western civilization to relate the "heavenly" and the "earthly" realms (*Engaging*, 4-6).

In the *ancient worldview*, "everything earthly has its heavenly counterpart, and everything heavenly has its earthly counterpart ... events initiated in heaven would be mirrored on earth." In many ways, this is the worldview of the Bible, especially apocalyptic literature, but it was also shared by many ancient peoples.

In the *spiritualistic worldview*, something else happens. The universe is firmly divided into spirit and matter, soul and body, and one part is set over against the other. This is the worldview of Platonism, Gnosticism, and Manichaeism, each of which profoundly influenced early Christianity. In this worldview, spirit or soul is good and matter or body is bad. Humans are spirits trapped within bodies, and the goal of salvation is to escape the material world to go "home" to heaven.

Partly in reaction against this view, the *materialistic worldview* developed. In this paradigm, there is a complete denial of anything beyond the senses. The spiritual world is deemed unreal, and only material existence has value. In its more extreme forms, this is the worldview of scientific reductionism, but it is also the functional cosmology of many Christians in the overdeveloped societies of the west, who have imbibed this worldview from birth.

While trying to salvage the "spiritual" aspects of faith without challenging the dominant scientific paradigm, theologians over the past several centuries have developed what Wink calls the *theological worldview*. In this paradigm, there is indeed a "supernatural" realm, which includes God and human souls, but this realm has virtually nothing to do with the "real world" known by the senses and investigated by modern science. (In the secular version of this worldview, the supernatural world is replaced by the realm of meaning, value, and aesthetics.) According to Wink "this view of the religious realm as hermetically sealed and immune to challenge from the sciences has been held not only by the Christian center and right, but by most of theological liberalism and neoorthodoxy".

In contrast to each of these previous worldviews, Wink

41

identifies the emergence of a new worldview being articulated by a number of different sources, including depth psychology, creation spirituality, process philosophy, quantum physics, and the new biology. This *integral worldview* "sees everything as having an outer and an inner aspect. It attempts to take seriously the spiritual insights of the ancient or biblical worldview by affirming a withinness or interiority in all things, but sees this inner spiritual reality as inextricably related to an outer concretion or physical manifestation." In this integral worldview, the spirit world is no longer "up there", but rather "within". These, of course, are both spatial metaphors; another way of putting it may be that spirit is to body as energy is to matter. In fact, in the integral paradigm, energy might be a more helpful term than spirit, as it has less "otherworldly" linguistic baggage. In any case, the heavenly realm (or spirit world) in this perspective is not separate from earthly material existence. Rather, it is the "depth dimension", the interiority, the inner energy of which all materiality is composed.

For Christian animism, this *integral worldview* provides a very helpful conceptual foundation. It helps us understand how every created being is both spirit and body, energy and matter. When we speak of the spirit of a tree, or the angel of an ecosystem, we do not mean something "extra", something essentially disembodied which then takes possession of an essentially inanimate object. Instead, we are referring to the "withinness" or depth dimension or energy of the being in question.

This *integral worldview* which Wink describes shares much in common with what is known as "systems theory". In systems theory, each being or entity in the universe is constituted by a complex pattern (or system) of smaller entities. At the same time, the entity itself is greater than the sum of its parts; it is a whole, not just an aggregate of smaller sub-systems. Each being is also itself a part of larger systems, wheels within wheels we might say. Systems theory is an important aspect of modern ecological thinking, which encourages us to see the world as complex webs of life, interrelated patterns within the whole.

A growing number of scientists and eco-philosophers, such as Ervin Laszlo, Gregory Bateman, and Freya Mathews, hold the opinion that consciousness is inherent within systems, and that all systems are conscious selves. Systems, at all levels, are characterized by flows of matter, energy, and information (or, in the older language, body, spirit, and mind). This means then, that spirit and consciousness are not limited to human individuals, but rather are characteristic of all beings, including cells, plants, animals, bioregions, ecosystems, the planet itself, and even solar systems and galaxies. Consciousness is no longer just the "ghost in the machine" which appears in humans alone, but is rather a phenomenon which is spread throughout the whole creation.

It takes some time to get used to looking at reality from a systems perspective. We are well trained by the reductionist materialist model to see ourselves and the rest of the world as little autonomous bits, unconnected to each other in any meaningful way. Living systems theory enables us to see ourselves, and all beings, as systems made up of smaller systems and part of larger systems; wheels within wheels within wheels. Of course, as theologians such as Wink would remind us, not all systems are healthy. Human social systems share in the human phenomenon of "fallenness". These systems are a bit like "fallen angels", created good, but warped into patterns of domination and control. These are the powers and principalities which shape so much of human existence, and which act like parasites or vampires within the host environment of ecological systems. The powers and principalities have a life of their own, beyond the individuals constituting them, as anybody working for social transformation instinctively knows.

This is all very abstract; let me give a concrete example. Saskatoon is a city. According to systems theory it is also a being, a living system made up of many subsystems and individuals bound together by shared flows of matter, energy, and information. Saskatoon is more than just a collection of its citizens and buildings – it has a life of its own. Furthermore, it is embedded in and contributes to larger systems such as the province, the nation, etc. It is also physically dependent on the surrounding bioregions, most notably the South Saskatchewan River, and the fertile plains and valleys between the two branches of the River (these are very basic contours; a complete mapping of the living system which is Saskatoon would be exceedingly complex). Wink would assert that Saskatoon is a principality, having an "inner spirit" which is manifested in its concrete day to day workings. It is also a fallen principality. That is not to say it is evil, but simply that as a human social system, Saskatoon shares in the human trait of fallenness. As well as being a life-giving and culture-sustaining place, Saskatoon is also a breeding ground for injustice, racism, and oppression within its walls, as well as exploiting and polluting the natural systems on which it depends. A principality is an ambiguous being indeed.

For a more comprehensive analysis of human socio-political systems, I would highly recommend Wink's trilogy on the powers and principalities, both for understanding the systems themselves and for nonviolent strategies on how to help transform the powers-that-be toward their divine vocation. But for now let us return to the spirits of the land, and our communion with them via the powerful processes of human imagination.

Visionary Communion and the Liberation of the Imagination

The "integral worldview" described above gives us a helpful conceptual framework as we attend to our experiences of the natural world as living, sentient, and personable. Let us be blunt: trees and animals don't talk. They don't speak words which strike our eardrums and are recognizable in English (or in Cree, for that matter!) What we are dealing with when we experience communion or communication with other life forms is a spirit-to-spirit interaction. For instance, I may wish to have a conversation with our community garden. So one evening, I go down to the garden, do a little weeding, and then sit down to meditate. As I clear my mind and quiet my heart, my spirit (energy) begins to interact with the spirit of the garden (remember, as a living system, the garden has an energy pattern, a spirit, a life of its own); picture two force fields "feeling each other out", exchanging energy and information.

On the human end of the exchange, much of the interaction remains semi-conscious. I may notice that I feel good after being in the garden for a while, but if I'm not paying close attention, I will not be aware that my spirit has actually been communing with another being. However, if I do pay attention, and know what to "look" for, I may begin to receive more conscious perceptions of the spirit of the garden. Intuitions may emerge about what the garden needs – a little more sunlight here, some compost over there please – that sort of thing. The spirit of the garden may try to draw my attention to other aspects of life unfolding around it, such as the skatepark down the hill, or the river, or the flock of birds above. The garden may share memories of what has been, or concerns about what is to come. All of these things are examples of what I might receive from an hour of visiting with the spirit of the garden.

And then one day, when the time is right and my spirit is wide open, I may go down to the garden to do some digging, a bit of fall cleanup. All of a sudden, the atmosphere shifts, a sense of surreality overtakes me, and there before me in the midst of my daughter's tomato vines stands a beautiful spirit-being, clothed as it were in tendrils of vegetation, feet rooted at the ankles in the soil of the garden. This is neither ghost nor demon, but rather the spirit of the garden itself. Communion now occurs not in the form of vague impressions or intuition, but rather in face-to-face communication.

Personally, I have never had such an intense encounter with a spirit, though I know others who have. The sceptic will find multiple ways to explain away such a phenomenon, but a Christian animist might interpret it like this: the energy field of the living system which is the garden is interacting with the energy field of the person working there. Information is being shared, spirit-to-spirit, with the human receiving this information at a semi-conscious level. Then at some point, for any number of different reasons, the spiritual (energetic) impressions break through from the subconscious mind to the active imagination (sometimes called the visionary perception) of the human. She looks up and "sees" the spirit-being in front of her. Is it "real"? Yes and no. No, in that it usually cannot be seen by others around her, and can probably not be tracked by most scientific instruments. But is it then "just" the seer's imagination? No, it is the actual spirit, or interiority, of the garden, a real being in and of itself. But the encounter which the human is having with the garden is being mediated by the active imagination of the seer.

The realm which is being perceived in an encounter such as this is not imaginary, but rather *imaginal*. "Imaginary" implies make-believe or unreal, whereas "imaginal" denotes a form of visionary consciousness, an ability to view the world at deeper layers than those perceived by ordinary consciousness. It is as if there is a layer of reality formed "between" the interwoven realms of energy and matter, a layer of consciousness which is home to mythic imagery and archetypal patterns. Perhaps this is the realm of Jung's "collective unconscious", or the famous "otherworld" of Celtic mythology. It is not the spirit-world itself (which is invisible energy), but rather the realm which "clothes" the spirit-world in culturally-specific imagery. A Cree elder and a Japanese artist might "see" the spirit of the garden in different forms, but both would be encountering the same living system which is the garden itself, from the "inside-out" as it were.

Throughout the ages, artists and storytellers have been mediators of such visionary forms of consciousness for the wider society. A good example of this is C.S. Lewis' portfolio of fantasy and science fiction. In his Narnia chronicles and his Ransom trilogy, Lewis introduces a wide variety of characters which are more-than-human. Most famous are the Talking Beasts of Narnia, but dancing in the background are also mythological beings such as fauns, centaurs, naiads, dryads, and even various non-Christian deities. For Lewis, these animistic characterizations are much more than just a clever literary device. Careful comparison with his nonfiction works and collections of his letters shows that Lewis believed that Nature has a life of her own, and that the multiplicity of created beings have their own integrity apart from any potential use for humans. (For a superb treatment of these ecological themes in Lewis' work, I would highly recommend *Narnia and the Fields of Arbol,* by Matthew Dickerson and David O'Hara. Similarly, Dickerson has also co-authored *Ents, Elves, and Eriador,* an exploration of the environmental thought embedded in Tolkien's Middle Earth.

Works of fantasy fiction are often able to present a vibrant and robust Christian animist worldview in a much more compelling way than a dry-ish essay such as my own. It is one thing to do the careful thinking-through of philosophical and theological analysis; it is something quite different to find oneself caught up in a swashbuckling quest to resist oppressive power and heal the wounded land, surrounded by a vast variety of more-than-human persons in a living landscape of magic and meaning. In our fact-obsessed culture, there is no shortage of rational and scientific data about imminent environmental collapse. But the facts don't seem to be sinking in. Rational arguments don't seem to have the power to effect the type of radical transformation which our culture requires to reverse our present dystopic trajectory. What is needed (among other things) is a liberation of the imagination. The Christian animism of Lewis, Tolkien, and others helps melt the winter of our hearts, caught in the "Jadis effect" of technological will-to-power.

I began this essay with a quotation from Tolkien's *Lord of the Rings,* describing the magnificence of the Tree-Shepherds, the Ents. Let me end with the voice of a dryad, a Narnian tree spirit in Lewis' *The Last Battle,* crying out for justice and deliverance from the oppressive regime of the false-Aslan:

"Woe, woe, woe!" called the voice. "Woe for my brothers and sisters! Woe for the holy trees! The woods are laid waste. The axe is loosed against us. We are being felled. Great trees are falling, falling, falling.

May our ears be opened to the cries of the trees, and the voices of creation all around us. May our hearts be transformed, and our imaginations liberated, that we might join with our more-than-human allies in a shared resistance against the ecocidal powers-that-be who seek to dominate the world. Above all, take heart: Aslan is on the move!

Works Cited

Bradley, Ian. *The Celtic Way*. London: Darton, Longman, and Todd, 1993.

DeWaal, Esther. *A World Made Whole*. London: Fount, 1991.

Hardin, Jesse Wolf. *Gaia Eros*. Franklin Lakes: New Page Books, 2004.

Kaza, Stephanie. 'To Save All Beings: Buddhist Environmental Activism' in *Engaged Buddhism in the West* . (Christopher S. Queen, ed.) Somerville: Wisdom Publications, 2000

Kinsley, David. *Ecology and Religion*. Englewood Cliff: Prentice Hall, 1995.

Lewis, C.S. *The Chronicles of Narnia*. New York: HarperCollins.

Maclean, Dorothy. *The Findhorn Garden*. New York: Harper and Row, 1975.

Macy, Joanne. 'The Greening of the Self' in *The Engaged Buddhist Reader* (Arnold Kotler, ed.) Berkeley: Parallax Press, 1996.

Nickelsburg, George, and James C. VanderKam. *1 Enoch: A New Translation*. Minneapolis: Fortress Press, 2004.

Seed, John, Joanna Macy, Pat Fleming, Arne Ness. *Thinking Like a Mountain: Toward a Council of All Beings*. Santa Cruz:

New Society Publishers, 1988.

Starhawk. *The Spiral Dance*. San Francisco: HarperSanFrancisco, 1989.

Tolkien, J.R.R. *Lord of the Rings: The Two Towers*. London: HarperCollins, 1991.

Wink, Walter. *Engaging the Powers*. Philadelphia: Fortress Press, 1992.

Wink, Walter. *Unmasking the Powers*. Philadelphia: Fortress Press, 1986.

CHRISTIAN
ALTERNATIVE

Throughout the two thousand years of Christian tradition there have been, and still are, groups and individuals that exist in the margins and upon the edge of faith. But in Christianity's contrapuntal history it has often been these outcasts and pioneers that have forged contemporary orthodoxy out of former radicalism as belief evolves to engage with and encompass the ever-changing social and scientific realities. Real faith lies not in the comfortable certainties of the Orthodox, but somewhere in a half-glimpsed hinterland on the dirt track to Emmaus, where the Death of God meets the Resurrection, where the supernatural Christ meets the historical Jesus, and where the revolution liberates both the oppressed and the oppressors.

Welcome to Christian Alternative... a space at the edge where the light shines through.